MY LIFE THROUGH POETRY EYES

BY MICHAEL JOHNSON JR.

MY LIFE THROUGH POETRY EYES

Copyright © 2021

All rights reserved. The reproduction or utilization of this work in whole or in part in any form by any electronic, mechanical, or other means, now known or hereinafter invented, including xerography, photocopying, and recording, or in any information storage or retrieval system, is forbidden without the written permission of the publisher, **Bleeding Ink Creatives, LLC.**

This is a work of Poetry written by author, **Michael Johnson Jr.** All poetry included in this book is a direct reflection of the authors creative expression, and not that of the publishing company.

Publisher: Bleeding Ink Creatives, LLC
Editor: Raechelle Fanny (of Bleeding Ink Creatives, LLC)
www.bleedinginkcreatives.com

Book Cover Photography: Jeff Dez'hommes of Dez'Noir Elite Photography

For Mature Adult Audiences Only

DEDICATION

To my grandparents and my beloved Ms. Scott
This is for you

INTRODUCTION

I'm not perfect
I have seen dark days and stormy nights
but it took me this long to truly see the light
I'm locked in a cage
Overthinking myself to sleep
Picturing me at a young age
Wondering how my life got this way
but then it hit me
It's not all my fault
It's how I was raised
These are the stories about my life
and how I became **Blaze**

MISSING YOU

Missing you
Is something I always seem to do
but not like this
This night something was different
We used to make love until we were finished
Here let me get to the dream before I forget it
I am lost in a fantasy
Having a love affair with a woman
that is no longer to be seen
She passed away a long time ago
but every night she feels real to me
I couldn't really see her face
but I knew it was her
I can't forget her smile
or the Way her lips taste
We were fooling around under covers
like it was part of our skin
and then suddenly the room started to spin
She gave me a sideway grin
It felt so cold
Then she glided to the sky
and I reached out saying please God no
I am sorry

I should've never let her go
It's all my fault
I should've kept her close
Tears began to flood my eyes
and I screamed I need you
My heart will not survive
She started to drift off
and then everything started to shake
I didn't want to wake
I knew what I must do
Something I had forgotten
and that's pay my respects to her grave
Letting our love drift off to heaven's gate
Dedications to a love I should've kept close
I love you

CHANGED MY LIFE FOREVER

This is the chapter
that changed my life forever
I've never been fond of cheating
but when I met this person
My heart was barely beating
You see
This girl I was with was not the same
She changed
We used to share our hearts
until she found a reason to rip us apart
I still tried hard to keep us together
but the more I fought
The more she gave up
I had no more tears
Nothing but pain for staying by her side
through all these years
I mean we had great times
but who doesn't in the beginning
The sex was great
but it was hard to eat
when I knew
someone else was sharing my plate
I finally left Staten island

and went back to where I was born
Then a few days later
I saw her on Instagram
She moved on
She was on a date
hair done, nails done, everything did
I was hurt
I called her phone and it rang one time
She answered and I went berserk
What are you doing
I thought we were going to make this work
She said he's only a friend
Don't make this into something it isn't
Goodnight
She hung up the phone
and I cried into a bottle of Hennessy
I tried to call her back
and it went straight to her answering machine
Now this is the part of the story
that changed my life forever
It was time for me to move on
and get past this stormy weather
That night
I text someone I had my eyes on forever

I am a fan of her work
and she's always shown me support
She's my Instagram crush
I hit her up in the DM
I told her my heart feels like it's about to burst
She said call me I'm up

INSTAGRAM CRUSH

I swear to God
When I heard her voice
My heart jumped for joy
We talked for hours while I sat on the porch
She made me smile
I forgot about the pain
and the tears that stained my cheeks
There was never a quiet moment
It felt like we were destined to speak
I know I'm a sucker for love
because she already had me weak
I asked her when we could meet
Before she could answer I said what about this week
She laughed and I tell you no lie
She came the very next day
On my birthday in a one-piece
She was the most beautiful person I've ever seen
She met my family and we went out to eat
The whole day was fantastic
I could not wait to get her home and under my sheets
but the night did not end that way
All we did was kiss and part ways
I was fine with that

My heart was going crazy
because I already pictured her being my lady
Don't laugh
When I got undressed and relaxed
I searched her page and found a picture of her
I took a screen shot and made her my screen saver

TAKE YOUR TIME

Take off all your clothes
Don't talk
Take your time
I want to admire every curve
I want to give your body everything it deserves
Touch right there
Rub it don't be scared
I want your fingers soaking wet
Dripping with essence
You got me so hard
I inch my way into your presence
Spread your legs so I can bury my face in it
My tongue plays no games
I eat and I don't want anything going to waste
Now I got you where I want you
Manmade lubricated
Now ready for deep penetration
I can feel the heat as I tickle in deep
I grab your hair and bring your body to me
I can feel your grips getting weak
I can hear your pussy starting to speak
As juices wet up the sheets
I got you next round on me

WHERE IS THE LOVE

Please I can't take anymore
It seems like day after day I get beat to the floor
Where is the love we used to share
All I feel is hate with angry tears
Night after night
You come home reeking of beer
You scream, yell and pull my hair
This is my life
I live in fear
I can't go outside
because there's always black & blue in my eyes
There's no one to call to stand by my side
It's hard to sleep
When death lays with me under my sheets
There's no passion
When he Rams me from the side
All I do is cry and wonder why
He used to love me
but now he's dead inside
There's no beat to his heart or shadow to his soul
He owns me and he will never let me go
{My words from a beautiful heart -
THANK YOU for letting me write your story}

NEVER FORGIVE YOU

I will never forgive you for what you've done
You took advantage of me when I was young
The thought of it now brings me to tears
So you all understand,
This woman made me into a man
Because of her I knew what was in my pants
and I used it on all my female friends
She turned me into a monster
A devil with no plan
I cannot get enough
Sex is always on my brain
I am a womanizer
I cannot be tamed
I fuck and I fuck
Every woman I meet
Just to hear them scream
When I'm inside them deep
Right now I'm in a serious relationship
and I don't want to cheat
Is it her fault or mine that I am a freak

MY LAST HOUR

There is a line that I have crossed
I have loved and I have lost
when I leave I am ghost
I feel pain so I turn to rain
Beautiful days seem to fade away
My emotions are forever drained
I take my pictures down
and burn them in the flames
This is my last hour
Soon you will forget my name
I closed my eyes before it hit my brain
Just so you know
I get high when my heart is in pain
This is not my choice
It runs in my veins
If I must die kill me today
because I cannot live another hour
Without my Sunrise or my Flower

SHE MAY LOVE YOU NOW

What more do you want from me
I have no more to give
You took my kid
and broke my heart
Now you want to come back into my life
Well, you can't
Cause' someone else has my soul
and she's been by my side holding me close
Helping wipe all the tears you put in my eyes
There are no more dark days
I can finally see the sunrise
There are no more pictures of us
I burned them all to dust
Let me see my daughter
If not, I'll wait until she grows up
and tell her the truth behind your lies
She may love you now
but she will hate you later
She will know what you did to me
You will burn in her eyes for your crimes

SLOWLY DRIFTING

I am slipping away
Slowly drifting
My heart cannot stand to take any more pain
I'm lost living in the flames
Feeling alone and drained
No one can save me
I'm already at my end
Every day I live in sin
Drugs and alcohol fog my mind
I have no more tears
I'm dying inside
I have been broken
and stripped of all my pride
I have four kids
and they don't even know that I'm alive

FADE AWAY

You faded me away and kicked me in the dirt
How am I supposed to move on
When you hit me where it hurts
My heart
Was supposed to be guarded in your hands
We had a future together
I thought our love would last to no end
but here I am
Crying over a heart that's not even beating
If you did care
You would've never been cheating
Right now
It's hard to hear your voice
Without breaking down and feeling defeated
I am a broken man
Without you I have no further plans
I sit here and cry my life away
Wishing I would die
So I won't be in pain another day
With tears in my eyes as I slowly fade away

DIAMOND IN THE ROUGH

In 1974 Minisa was born
She had it rough
but she never gave up
Even when all hope was gone she remained strong
Minisa could not be broken down
She did everything on her own
I know her struggle
and it weighs heavy on my soul
That's why when I hold her
I never let her go
Minisa has a heart of gold
and whoever hurt her needs to die slow
She is a beautiful woman with two amazing kids
Even through her strokes and the pain that she suffered
Minisa always finds the strength to take care of others
That's why my heart will always love her

{Dedication: Minisa soon to be Mrs. Johnson}

WHY I WRITE

My heart is constantly in pain
There's never a quiet moment
Always thunder before the rain
I'm tired of living in the dark
It's time for me to step into the light
Release my scars
and show the world my life is no game
This will be my legacy
I don't want to be a lost memory
I want my kids to know the truth behind my insanity
I've been through hell and back
I still live in madness
but when I write I get lost in a zone
and I let go
Of what's buried beneath the surface of my soul

HATEFUL VOICES

I shall never live in fear again
of hateful voices that cloud my mind with sin
Just know
All those who crossed me will feel the wrath of my pen
I will not use violence
I am a changed man
but if you bring it to my front door
No words
I'll lay your back on the floor

SILENTLY I SLEEP

Silently I sleep
Dreaming of life
and how it used to be

I deeply miss my friends
Even the girls that used to lay in my bed
Although some of them turned into enemies
I still miss the love in between their legs

Silently I sleep
Dreaming of life
and how it used to be

I had my first child and I was so proud
I rushed home every day so I wouldn't miss a sound
He looks like me
but with his mother's complexion
I just wish I could start over again

Silently I sleep
Dreaming of life
and how it used to be

My mother used to tuck me in
and shield me from harm

She'd tell me she loves me and that I was her charm
   but when I was broken where were her arms
  It seems like now she can only love me from afar

UNCONTROLLABLE SPASMS

I cannot see
I cannot breathe
I'm stuck in hell for eternity
No one can wake me
No one can save me
My bones are shaking and my heart is aching
I try to cry
but nothing forms in my eyes
I try to scream
yet no sound follows me
I'm in too deep
Is this real or is this a dream
Darkness surrounds me
There's nothing under my feet
The walls of despair are closing in around me
The depth of my depression is suffocating me
All of a sudden I hear my name
and like a beast I fight through the pain
Forcing myself to come undone
I finally arise with my loved one by my side

BROKEN GLASS

Me
What Have you done for me
Besides bring in reinforcements to take me to jail

Her
You deserve it
Because living with you is like a nightmare from hell

Me
What are you talking about
This is what I mean
I come home from work
and the house is not even clean
There is no dinner on the table
and your eyes are full of steam
All you do is get high and blame it on me

Her
I want to leave

Me
So go!
I already threw your heart out the door
I don't even know why you're still here
There is no love only tears

You come home around 6:00 in the morning
Covered in sweat
Like you were running around whoring

Her

I do not care what you think
This is my life and I can write it with my own ink

Me

She leaves
I am left with disfigured words
and a heart that is profoundly disturbed
Before this all got started we were the perfect match
I remember when I met her
She was as delicate as a feather
with the lips and eyes of an Angel
I gave her everything she ever wanted
She always wanted more
and I gave it to her because behind closed doors
She fucked and sucked me until I was sore
I kept her spoiled and she became rotten
Like an apple right down to her core
If she did not get what she wanted
She would put a lock on her drawers
Some nights she'd be missing for hours
and her phone would be off

When I asked her about it she would lie with no flaws
My Angel became my devil
My worst fear became my life
She said I pushed her to drugs
but I know she is playing with words
Whatever she's doing out there
Has her emotionally disturbed
She deliberately gets mad at me
So she can leave and run the streets
but I love her so much that I'll be right here
With tears of pain ripping down my cheeks
We do this every Friday of every week
I cannot let her go
My heart is too weak

SATISFIED

Even though she was not mine
and her heart was taken
She still let me in between her thighs
Every time her man was vacant
I did not care
Just as long as she left me satisfied
Whenever she rang my bell
There were always tears in her eyes
I told her everything she wanted to hear
and kissed away her fears
I got her undressed
I know what she needs
So I dive headfirst with my tongue in the lead
It's hard to imagine someone not keeping her pleased
Because every lick I take
makes My taste buds scream
I pray he keeps hurting her
So she keeps running back to me
With open legs where my tongue wants to be

THERE'S ONLY ONE WAY TO FORGIVE

I do not want to waste any more time
Get undressed and move those panties to the side
I want to feel inside you
So turn around and bend on all four
I'm going to give you every inch of me
So deep and so raw
I need to release this fire that runs through my veins
There's no taking it slow
I want the neighbors to hear my name
I truly am sorry
Because you are a victim of my heart being in pain
I have no one else to take it out on
I will not stop until all of me is completely drained
Then I will go back home and forgive her again

MY HOPES AND DREAMS

I'm not different
MLK and my dreams are the same
No matter if I'm right or wrong
I still beat my drums, stomp my feet
and present everyone with a multi-racial speech
In this world now the hate is too deep
There's no fixing the cracks in the street
We are divided and we will fall
We fight against each other for what cause
Because of the color of our skin
There will be no winners at the end of this war
Just victims and dried blood on the floor
Broken hearts that cannot cry anymore
Regardless of our religion
We are one nation under God
and I have faith that we will change
So the next generation
Will not have to live in our flames

I WOKE UP

I woke up today
with a funny feeling in my heart
I knew where it came from
but it still set me apart
I was in love
but with every beat
It dripped with pain
I tried to relax
I felt so drained
What did I do last night that got me feeling this way
I slowly started to remember
I was drinking and partying
because of an argument I had with my woman
It pushed me to escape
She was playing with fire
and I did not want to keep calling her hateful names
She deserved every minute of it
because she was week between the legs
and needed to pay for her mistake
Taking her back does not mean I forgave her
She was just the mother of my child
She expected our love to stay the same
I tried

It changed
When I pictured him in her eyes it drove me insane
and it was time for her to feel my pain
So last night I brought someone home
The only thing I was waiting for
Was her knock on my door

I'M NOT GETTING ANY YOUNGER

There are no more mistakes for me
I can't keep running around
Sticking my love in every woman
that gives me a smile
Being who I was is over
It's time to settle down
and calm my heart from sexual sounds
Please try to understand me
I am at that age
I just want to be a part of a family
I'm tired of running the streets
Chasing women
Getting high off unrequited love
They take all my passion
but do not know me underneath
I just want one woman for the rest of my life
To hold me under the sheets
I want to share one heartbeat
Walk hand in hand
and grow with the same shadow
As I become more of a man
I want her to know me like she knows herself
and never be insecure because she knows her wealth

I will only have eyes for her and I know I'm not perfect
When I see her smile
I know she is worth it

MIRROR

When I look in the mirror
I see a reflection of myself
but something is different
I'm not the same person I once was
I let them change me
They took bits and pieces of my soul
and rearranged my way of thinking
If I did fall in love I'd lose control
because I'm always thinking about being hurt
Truthfully
I cannot go back to being in pain
I have scars that never healed
and my tears will forever rain
I closed everyone off
and tied my heart with an unbreakable chain

I LOVE YOUR SMELL

I want to break up
but I'm in love with your smell
You have a hold on me
and it keeps me impelled
It's like the lights are off but you always find a way
To let me see your light through the stormiest days
You wrap me in your arms
and I can smell your essence leaking from your skin
You melt away all my pain
With a taste I cannot explain
I fight back the tears
and push the hate out of my veins
I get lost in your passion
as I move deeper into your cave
Flashes of memories have me wanting to escape
but my body wants more
So I turn you around and eat every hole
Until you are dripping with gold
Then I close my eyes and bury my nose
I inhale deeply
Your scent traps me completely
You are the best because you know how to keep me

ONE DAY

One day
I will be your King
One day
You will be my Queen
Our lives will never be the same
From the first moment I met you
Until the day you went away
I was in love with your smile
and the way your eyes met my gaze
You are enchanted into my soul
and I don't ever want to let you go
One day
Our hearts will intertwine
One day
There will be no more tears to hide that smile
I do not know if he hurts you
or fills your heart with lies
but I've been in pain
I know how it feels to stay in a relationship
and be completely drained
If you need me to take you away
Just whisper my name
and I will cross the Verrazano like a runaway slave

One day
You'll be mine
One day
the world will close its eyes
If I never get to have you
I'll keep you in my dreams
You'll be the only fantasy I'll ever need
You are the lock
and I am the key
I genuinely want to love you for eternity
Even when we are old and grey
that fire I have for you now
will never burn away.

NO LOVE
A Duet

Her
I can't keep pretending
That we're going to make this work
There's no happy ending
If we stay we both will be hurt

I ripped my heart out and buried it in the dirt
You will never find it or feel my love again
because we were drowning in waters
Too deep for us to swim
You fed me lies
and I pushed you dreams
You made me cry
and I fed your pride
You cheated
and I got no revenge
True story
Do you think you are more of a man
because you blacken my eyes like the ink in my pen
Your hands are stained with my blood and my tears

There is no love that comes with fear
I stayed
because our bond was rare
Not because of what we shared under the sheets
but because of who you used to be
You treated me like a Queen
until the devil came in between

I was your diamond in the rough
Until you found Crystal on the side
Even when we used to walk outside
You made me feel like trash
Cause' every woman that walked past
You turned around and looked at her ass
I felt so unwanted
How can you say you love me
and want me to be your wife
You put me in a predicament
I want to kill you or die trying
You are the only man
That put scars on my heart too big to stitch
I cannot wait
Cause' payback's a bitch

NO LOVE

Me

You took my pride
I have no more tears
I just want to pack my bags and slowly disappear
You are a liar
Someone who manipulates others
To make it seem like I am an abusive lover
All I did was give you my heart
and you took advantage of me
That is what pushed us apart
Truthfully
I never cheated
I just wanted to see you in pain
For all those nights you kicked me out in the rain
and I sat on the porch feeling like you had me trained
My life is no game
You cannot keep torturing my soul
and spitting on my name

There is no love that comes with fear
I stayed because our bond was rare
and not because of what we shared under the sheets
but because of who you used to be

You treated me like a King
until the devil came in between

Then you changed
I could see it in your eyes
the same way you used to look at me
is how you look at other guys
You broke me into pieces
and just for the record
I knew you were weak between your thighs
and your lips were being used for passion on the side
but it's alright because we have no ties
I can easily leave any day without saying goodbye

I can't keep pretending
That we're going to make this work
There's no happy ending
If we stay we both will be hurt

WHAT WE HAD

I'm not going to front
When I see you on social media
I miss what we had
I see he makes you happy
and for some reason I made you sad
I do not understand
What is going on in your mind
but if you press rewind
Does it put tears in your eyes
I know it's my fault for leaving you behind
but I had to hit the streets
Grind and climb
To the top
Money, sex and gun smoke
Kept me from coming home
and when I finally got up
I forgot who held me close
So I pushed you away and turned you into a ghost
I know I hurt your heart
and melted your soul
I scarred you so deeply
You couldn't take me back
Under the sheets completely

and when you did
You closed your eyes and cried
You took hold of me and said
Don't ever leave my side
I said I promise
I will love you until the end of time
but that was a lie
I knew you felt it under your skin
because you kissed me goodbye
Like you would never see me again

A SLAVE UNDER COVERS

I was trapped and I wanted to escape
but she had me by the collar
She controlled my fate
I loved her but I had to get away
cause each and every day
She was pumping Poison into my veins
Nothing felt the same
Not even her touch
I could not stand to lay next to her
Let alone be deep in her guts
I didn't trust her
There were always lies that came to my mind
Even though her body was fine
It was her heart I really wanted
but every night I was her slave under covers
and that's where I took my anger out
She loved it
So I pulled her hair
I choked her until she had no more air
I tied her up and ripped her apart
I did everything I wanted to do without the abuse
I beat the pussy until it was blue
but she did not have a clue

That there was pain and tears in my eyes
The only thing she cared about was being satisfied
and when I came
I was emotionally drained
I went to sleep on my side cursing her name

I GAVE

Who am I
but a lost soul walking on a thin line of love and hate
Was it me
Is it my fault that everyone I loved walked away
How can I live with myself
When I love so much but it is never enough
I gave and I gave
Until my heart fucking caved
I trusted to be betrayed
I spend most of my days in a mist of poetry and haze
I write in a cycle of sadness and pain
My memories will never be the same
I'm forced to live in this madness
The abuse will never fade
No one deserves to feel what I have taken
I am a wounded man broken and shaken

HATERS

Truth be told
Haters gon' hate but tomorrow there'll be fans
You may not like my wife
or think of me as being less of a man
because I choose to write my emotions
With tears in my pen
I'm never going to change who I am
I'm going to rise to the top
With or without you
There's no stopping me
When I lose control my mind blacks out
and I get lost in another world
I can see the scars
I can feel the pain
So I write my soul and release it from its cage
Excuse me
If I know how to articulate my words better than most
Talk about me all you want
Just turn the next page...

NO MORE FORGIVENESS

You put pain in my heart
Too many times
There is no more forgiveness
Just erase my last name
and stay the hell out of my business
There is no love for you
Anywhere swimming in my soul
What we had is dead and gone
but the love of my child still stays strong
Go ahead keep feeding her lies
You are not just hurting me
When you bring tears to her eyes

BLOOD SUCKERS

I lay silently in a grave
because I was once a slave of poetry in pain
My days and nights were filled with hatred and rage
I could not breathe
Those blood suckers were killing me
I had to escape
because they kept playing dangerous games
They kicked me when I was down
but fucked me when I was up
They had me at the end of my chains
and I knew if I broke loose
I would've burned them to flames
Pissed on their ashes
and called them out by their names
I am emotionally drained
So right now
Let me sleep a couple more years
I will rise with My Life through poetry eyes

NAKED

Under the fabric of my clothes
There's something beyond words
I know how to please your soul
Hold me and don't let go
I can take the pain away and rearrange your heart
I can show you what real love feels like
When we are naked in the dark
and our bodies collide
Leaving wetness between your thighs
As I glide gently inside
I'm going to give you as much of me as you can take
Until you lock me deep inside your safe

BREAKING DOWN

Entangled in my own thoughts
I can't seem to get my head straight
I'm breaking down like an earthquake
There is no shelter to hide my tears
There's no one around to hear my heartbeat that cares
I wander the world with fear
It's hard to smile when pain dwells
Agony is my first name
I'm just a walking soul
That no one seems to know
It's all her fault but if this is what it must be
I have to embrace my fate
That I will die alone old and gray
because I cannot see a brighter day
My life is engulfed in flames
That never seemed to burn away
I'm shattered into pieces
I live on emptiness
I do not eat
and it's hard for me to sleep
I'm scared to get trapped in my dreams
because everything is never what it seems
One minute I'm happy

and the next I'm filled with rage
Then I wake up in an emotional spin
and it leaves me wondering
If I should forgive her again

PEACE OF MIND

When I see your face my emotions escape
The memories will never fade
I was locked in your cage
Heart beating with rage
Love is a dangerous game and you will never change
Fuck living in flames
While I'm burning up all your pictures
Your smile is tantalizing my senses
I'm being betrayed by visions
I can't believe I oversaw your commitment
Stop begging me for forgiveness
This was your decision
Please stop screaming like you're the victim
You're crying just for attention
You lied from the beginning
Your heart was always missing
I hope that you are listening
Cause' someone else took your position
She kissed away all my pain
and ever since I met her
I don't even remember your name

ZENITH

When I love

my heart is always at its highest peak

When I get hurt it really cuts me deep

I know no one's perfect

and everybody is not meant to be

but goddamn

Let me have a chance at true romance

Let her be the Angel that sits on my shoulder

Let her be the high when my heart is feeling sober

I hope that I find her before my life is over

I DON'T WANT TO BE TOUCHED

I do not want to be touched
I do not want to be loved
I do not need your kisses
I do not need your hugs

Stay away from me
You've already done enough
There's nothing you can say to earn back my trust
You lied and lied
I forgave and forgave
This time not me but you will pay for your mistakes

I do not want to be touched
I do not want to be loved
I do not need your kisses
I do not need your hugs

You never cared
If you did
I would not be heartbroken pouring out tears
Get away from me because once again
You thought with no Fear
There's no reason to keep holding on

When your love really isn't there

I do not want to be touched
I do not want to be loved
I do not need your kisses
I do not need your hugs

There's nothing to talk about
Get out of my house
The longer you are here
The more I want to pop you in your mouth
Stop trying to hold me
Pack your bags before I make your shit trash

I do not want to be touched
I do not want to be loved
I do not need your kisses
I do not need your hugs

HEART OF GOLD

There was once a lonely girl with a heart of gold
She ran the streets nightly inducing her soul
No one could contain her
She was beautifully out of control
I cannot believe she is gone
The memories will always live on

Rest in Peace
To My Heart of Gold

CONOCEMOS LA VERDAD

There is madness in your heart
and you try so hard to blame me for your scars
We both know the truth is written in the dark
I will shine the light and show the world
How fucked up you truly are

DAISY

She loves me
She loves me not

She sneaks away when my eyes are closed
There is no loyalty within her soul
She lies to my face
Then cries when I'm ready to go
She begs me to stay and my heart always folds

She loves me
She loves me not

I woke up every morning
With my heart in knots
So she took it upon herself to kiss me
and climb on top
I wanted to push her off but her body was so soft
It felt so good to be inside that I wanted to cry

She loves me
She loves me not

That night I was her fool

She used my emotions like I was a tool
Her passion aside
She's got me confused
I'm stuck in love and I don't know what to do

She loves me
She loves me not

CURSED

There is no hope for me
I am cursed to live in these flames
When I sleep she touches my dreams
and when I wake up she is right here
Pretending to be my Queen
There is no letting her go
She will take everything I have
and still stomp on my soul

FOLLOW MY WORDS

Hopefully when they mention my name
They don't tell lies to tarnish my fame

When I die
Tell my kids the truth
Let them know their dad was not a fool

I have scars deep on my heart
Either help me
or leave me in the dark

Make me laugh
I hate to be sad
Show me love or kiss my ass

I am black
With caramel skin
If you get one taste you'll come back again

If I open my door
Take off your shoes and don't hurt my heart
because I'm not in the mood

I am thirty-six with a fire in my eyes
and hunger in my soul
Don't run away when I need you the most

WHY CRY

She said

Why cry

When my heart belongs to you

Because you've been through so much

Yet still, you ride

I never got a chance to appreciate

How perfect you are inside

She said

Why cry

Because a beautiful heart deserves no scars

I am sorry for letting my pride push you so hard

She said

Why cry

Because as I look into your eyes

I see tears of an Angel

You are a gift and right now

I just want to kiss your lips

She said

Why cry

When your heart belongs to me

FUTURE

I see wedding bells
and a heart that no longer dwells
I see us holding hands
Making love on endless sand
Beautiful nights are never wasted
and your lips are forever tasted
Every morning I wake up
My body craves your sexual fragrance
I know everything you like
and you have everything I need
If this is my future
I can't wait to see you as my queen
First, wishing we could get rid
of the heartaches in between

PAST

This is not going to work
You nag too much and your insecurities
Are only making this worse
You push me and I push back
We have nothing in common
Since I put a ring on your finger
It has been nothing but drama
Full fights in the kitchen
Using hateful words I will not mention
You kicked me out
Then I plead for your love
You took me back and I held a grudge
This cannot be my life
and I cannot see you as my wife
If we cannot fix what's broken
No words will be spoken
I will leave and you will not even know it

PRESENT

I never thought we would make it this far
It took me getting locked behind bars
To build a friendship we never had
and release the scars of our past
I never meant to make you cry
Anger and resentment pushed you to the side
We've both done a lot of nitpicking
and left our door open
for family members to start backbiting
We overcame the hate
and moved our hearts to a better place
Now I know what makes you smile
Your commitment to love makes me proud
You are my queen
The Angel of my dreams
My diamond in the rough
Without the heartache in between

MISTAKES AND LOVE

Me

I still have a lot more love to release

Her

I must go
If I don't go home he will beat me
Then kick me and my child on the streets

Me

I don't understand
Why you put up with this man
All he does is torture your soul
and spit on your plans

Her

I must go

Me

Wait!
Just give me a couple more minutes
to hold you close

Her

Why are you doing this

Me

Because I love you
and fuck him I need you the most
I swear to God
If he puts his hands on you again

Her

Stop!
This is not what I wanted
I mean
I love feeling you deep inside my stomach
but that is as far as you go
Don't get attached to me
That will only make my situation worse
I'm sorry I must leave
I have to get back to my gift and my curse

Me

I do not know what to do
I'm stuck between being in love and being a fool
I do not think I can save her

She is too in touch with being abused
I don't want to force her to pick and choose
What we have leaves me confused
When she walks out my door
My heart breaks in two
When I dream
I see her face
There is nothing I can do but stay in my place
and be there for her when he makes mistakes

I MISS YOUR TOUCH

I know you got my messages
and flowers I left at your door
I know you are still crying
and your heart is feeling torn
If you answer your phone
I can explain what I did wrong
We can try to fix this before all the fire is gone
As I'm writing down this letter
I'm writing with tears in my pen
I know you will never believe me
but that woman is just a friend
I'm not going to lie
I had feelings for her once upon a time
but since I've met you
She hasn't crossed my mind
We only met up
because she was feeling under the weather
She says I'm the only one that knows her better
Most of the time I talked about you
and she about her man being unfaithful
Even when she started to cry
I did not reach over the table
I just told her it will be alright

and that sometimes
A good woman deserves to be single
So she can appreciate herself
and understand their wealth
Not once did I cross the line
and try to make her my lover on the side
Whatever your friends told you
Those bitches are lying
I understand what I did was wrong
Please my love
Let me come home

DOWN TO MY BONES

They shook me until I was empty
They unearthed me and watched me bleed

I gave up so much of my life
To ungrateful women that didn't care if I lived or died
My mother once told me she'd never seen
so many tears pour from one man's eyes
She said I needed to change my taste
and stop chasing beauty living in disguise
I never listened
I guess I'm the type of guy
That doesn't know where true love lies
Even if it's right in my face
I will look the other way
because all it takes is a big butt and a smile
Then I'm right back in the same place

They shook me until I was empty
They unearthed me and watched me bleed

This will be my last time
trying for a healthy relationship
If this doesn't work out

I'm going to need a doctor quick
because I cannot take this anymore
My heart is already on the floor
I'm too good of a man to be getting shook to my core
I have no more leaves left
I'm down to my bones

BABY CAKES

Let me know if I'm going too far
but I know you like it
Especially in the back seat of your car
You are my trigger
My erotic ebony with a thousand scars
I love it when I tie you up so you can't run
and let you suck me off
Filling your mouth with all my cum
Then I eat until my tongue goes numb
Party time is every night
Different lingerie pussy tasting like water
I'm not going anywhere
and I put that on my daughters
You got me
Forever you will get my full potential
Back shots so deep
I'll make it feel like I'm tearing your tissue
Your back door I do adore
You tell me to choke you before I explore
Although it's once in a while
When you tell me you're ready
It always makes me smile

THE STREETS WASN'T THERE

I took nothing serious
I lived with no fear
because I couldn't be what I wanted to be
I ran the streets with no care
I started selling drugs at a young age
and made it my career
I had everything I ever wanted
Sex, money and cars
I had a good life until I got locked behind bars
This was my first felony
He hit me with two years
and I learned nothing from it
When I got released
I grinded even harder
I needed no sleep
I wanted everything
I was a beast
Staten Island is my home
It fed me
It showed me love
Until that day I went back in front of the judge
He smacked me with four years
and my heart stopped

Everything went silent
All I could think about was my money
and who the hell was telling
There was nothing I could do
Except do my time
Hoping the streets stay by my side
but once I got sent upstate
The streets buried me alive

LET GO

Don't say you love me
When there's so much pain underneath
Trust me this will not work
If you're already planning for defeat
My goal was not to hurt you
but I could feel you tormenting me
Like a shadow to my soul
Your silence breaks me apart
You are infamy to my already tainted heart
I am no stranger to the dark
Please let me go
Before my heart starts to explode
I want to be with you forever
but your eyes are still closed

BROKEN

My heart was broken when you lost your way
There was nothing I could do to get you to stay
You were free
Like the birds and the bees
and I was locked in chains with the devil at my feet

MCKENZIE

That beautiful little girl did not have to die
She was so close to my heart
I treated her like one of mine
I can still see her face when I close my eyes
Although we broke up
You could've given her to me or my cousin Ty
She was only five
When you took your daughter's life
So you could run the streets and be somebody's slide
You are insane and I hope you fucking fry
because McKenzie didn't deserve to die

PASSION FOR YOUR EYES

I don't know you
but I see passion in your eyes
Let me ask you one question
How long will it take me to get between your thighs
Bury my tongue
and make every part of your body come alive

I'M SORRY

What have I done
I left her with tears and a loaded gun
I cannot fix this
There is no way I can erase all that I have done
She will not forgive me
You should have heard her
There was so much hate pouring off her tongue
Her heart split in two
because she found out my life wasn't true
I should have never taken her hand
If I wasn't ready to be a faithful man

SHADOWS IN THE DARK

What kept us together
Is slowly tearing us apart
Once two lonely souls drifting in the dark
We found each other and healed our hearts
There was less talk and more sex
There were more smiles with no stress
We were the perfect match
but now we argue more than we kiss
I should leave but I can't let it end like this
I must find a way
To set fire back into our empty space

I'M NOT A FOOL

You must think I'm a fool
I can read through your lies
This is not the first time
I've seen treachery in my lover's eyes
but it's cool
As long as I get to take my kids to school
I will be right by your side
Until they are old enough to decide

ARGOT

We are one in the same
I know when you need passion
and I know when you are in pain
We share a special language
That no one could ever understand
That's why
I fall in love with you over and over again

WHITE LIES

I love you and I need you by my side
Without you I would never survive
There are still so many holes
Left open in my soul
Sometimes I forget
Who I'm talking to on the phone
In my defense
Your little white lies irk my nerves
If you mean nothing by it
Why try to hide it
I trust you
but put yourself in my shoes
What would you do
If you thought I was untrue
Would you leave me because of fear
or would you want me to reassure you
Every day that my love will never disappear

HELP

Beautiful pictures
but we are dead inside
She says she loves me
but I know we will never survive
Blinded by passion mixed with too many lies
I can't keep moving forward
With so many tears crawling behind
Please God show me a sign
Give me a reason to keep on trying
because even her touch is slowly dying
I need your help
I'm tired of crying

I MUST SAY GOODBYE

This is the end
There's no more back and forth
I'm tired of the abuse
because it's only getting worse
Nothing could've prepared me for this
One minute you're my angel
and the next you're a deranged bitch
I sleep with one eye open
and my heart is completely frozen
I can't go another night
With your trivial explosions
You're built around death
A woman without a soul
You will not kill me before I get old

EVERY NIGHT

I am a hot mess
I drink every night to relieve my stress
It never works
because my heart was ripped out of my chest

I cry every night because I plot my own death
People see me
but the ones I love spit on my success

She tells me every night
that I will never amount to anything
and she regrets the day
I put a baby in her stomach

Every day I write and it's not for the fame
It's to let the people of the world understand my pain
Hopefully taking what is needed
To change their fate before it's too late

CRAZY

You cannot have what does not belong to you
Even if I leave her tomorrow
I still wouldn't run to you
You've got me fucked up
Just because I like your pictures
Doesn't mean I like your features
I'll never give up a dime
for someone that only looks good from behind
I was about to go seven thirty
but that would be a waste of time
We never text
I've never heard your voice
You are a stalker in pain
and you will not drive me or my family insane

SECRETS

I hate to be lied to
Especially by someone I gave my life to
I can see it in her eyes
and I can feel it in her heart
Something is going on
and she's keeping it in the dark
Whatever it is
Is tearing me apart

FIEND

Get off of me
You're making a scene
You're not the same woman
That I once had as my queen
You're devilish
You will not get me to cheat
I just want to spend time with my daughter
Without you being a fiend

ADDICTED TO SIN

I gave up years ago
but she still tries to consume my soul
I had to stay away
because I could not tell if she was friend or foe
Now I know she was playing for the other side
Wishing for my downfall
There is no mistaking it
I can tell
by the way she keeps screaming my name
She is filled with hatred and rage
because I moved on and my life has changed
I was addicted to the taste of her passion
She had a hold on me
Every morning and every night I had to have it
I paid the price
Everyone I loved left my side
and I did stupid things to put tears in their eyes
I had no pride
I was dead to the world
but I got strong
I channeled all my desires into my poems
I just want to say
To the ones I pushed away

She is gone
I poured her down the drain
My heart will never beat for her again
Forgive me
I was addicted to sin

THINK OF ME

Have you ever
Woken up in the morning horny as fuck
To find no one by your side
Well let me help you with that
Start by rubbing that pussy side to side
Until it comes alive
Then drive your fingers deep inside
You can think of me
If that's how it must be
but you can't use two fingers
You would have to use three

REBORN

I wish you could take my pain away
and teach me what I need to change
Every time I find love
I'm back standing in the rain
Just take my life and bury me into a grave
My heart can't endure anymore games
What is the purpose of me being tortured
Where is it written that I truly deserve this
If this is a lesson I already paid for it
when you let them bitches
Take my sons and my daughters
My past is my past it's not my fault
Michael is back
I am reborn
I just need you to open your arms
Hold me close
Erase the memories I try so hard to hide
Defeat the demons that dwell inside
I raise my hand high
and I pray for your love to return to my veins
Please
Wash away all my sins
So I may find happiness again

HIS LOSS

I know it will take more than words
To give you everything you deserve
My eyes are wide open
I know how to control your emotions
I can take the pain away
Lay back and relax
Let my tongue feel the motion
I know how to heal your heart
I want to take you out of the dark
and make you release
So you can finally see the light
There will be no more tears
I can make you into a new woman
One that does not live in fear
You don't ever have to be scared again
Just read the words I write with my pen
You are beautiful from head to toe
You don't need to be with a man
That can easily let you go
It's not your loss it's his
Cause' when I find you
I will take your breath away
and make love to you each and every day

SHAME ON ME

Shame on me
For letting you push me away from my family

Where do I go
Now that I'm all alone
All the alcohol is gone
and my heart is wrapped in thorns
I could taste the tears and feel the pain
I want to take you back
but I know you will never change

Shame on me
For being a fool and a victim to your insanity

You tortured me with lies
and killed me with passion
You're sick in the head
More than I ever imagined
You stepped out on me and I am to blame
I hope you burn in hell
So I can piss out your flames

Shame on me

For shedding a tear for a heart that never cared

It's ok
because God made a way to ease my pain
I still feel ashamed for being betrayed
All I ever wanted
Was a love as pure as rain
but you taught me a valuable lesson
I will not make that mistake again

BEING A WOMAN

I am traditional in the sense of
Family, loyalty, and love
I'm a mother, daughter, wife
I'm all of the above
I am a child of God
I am beautiful inside and out
I am to be appreciated for my intellectual mind
Before you get to know my sensual side
I am light within my smile
I shine bright
To have me is to acquire a precious diamond
Unbreakable simply defined
I am a pillar of strength and a rock for my family
Put that together
Me and my man become complete
From the depth of my soul
I am unique in the sense of my growth
and getting to know me
I am a woman and a woman is who you will see

Contributing Author
My Queen, Minisa Johnson - @diamondmamipoems

BEING A MAN

Being a man
Means knowing what comes first
To live a life of love, not hate
Being a man
Means being headstrong
but also knowing how and when
To admit when he is wrong
Being a man
Means being the hero of his household
When everyone else is scared
He is the one that is bold
Being a man
Means not being afraid to ask for help
and with the choices he makes
He is secure within himself
Being a man
Means knowing when to sacrifice
When everyone else is doing wrong
He sets the tone by doing right
A man doesn't need the approval of others
He also knows that a man could not be a man
Without the love of his mother
Being a man

Means knowing his place
Always keeping his family safe and understanding
That he is nothing without God's grace
Letting no 'I love you' go to waste
I've explained the best I can
This is my interpretation of being a man

RAINDROPS

Who do I call when raindrops fall
and I'm soaking in pain with no one to call

I tried my best
I'm not perfect
I have flaws under the surface
Inside my heart beats a man
That only wishes to be loved again
Please forgive me for all my sins
Please forgive me for what I write with my pen

Who do I call when raindrops fall
and I'm soaking in pain with no one to call

I gave up years
Too many heartbreaking tears
The memory will never disappear
I am alone and I live in fear
Who is going to help me with tenderness and care
I need a touch or a whisper of love
I'm tired of looking to the stars above
This is my soul and my soul to keep

HEART TO HEART

What I cannot see
Will stay in the dark
HEART to HEART

When I sleep
It's the only time I find peace
HEART to HEART

When you kiss me
I fade in and out of pain
HEART to HEART

When will I learn
That your love will never take a faithful turn
HEART to HEART

When I look in your eyes
I see death in disguise
yet I stay
Knowing that I will never survive
HEART to HEART

You push and push me way too far

If I did not have kids
I would be locked behind bars
HEART to HEART

SCREAMING FOR AFFECTION

I love it when you get naked
and your body's screaming for affection
You know I'm the only one to finesse it
I take my time with these words
Like I take my time with those curves
I eat away all your pain
Hold me and don't let go
I promise you will explode
Your eruption will be heard
I follow your every motion
My tongue will get lost in your ocean
I'll drink up all your emotions
and take you to different places
Your heart rate will be unstable
as juice leaks from your lips
I lick it up and say thank you
For letting me take you to perfection
When your body was screaming for affection
and you know I'm the only one to finesse it

DON'T FEEL ALONE

I remember a time when love was warm
Now I sleep alone
Empty and cold
I gave so much and gained so little
My heart is torn
Ripped down the middle

Do not feel alone!

How can I not
When the one I loved left me to rot
I know I was there
I saw your commitment
but what you hold inside
Should be replaced with forgiveness

I would rather die
Than to let her see the tears in my eyes
and who are you to speak
but a conscience that feeds off grief
It's her fault not mine that she decided to cheat
When I never left her hungry under my sheets
Her doing this cut me deep

Then to leave with him shattered my dreams

Listen
Get rid of the dark side
Swallow your pride
Although she hurt you your soul still survived
To forgive is to conquer and she will realize
She pushed a good man to the side
For something she wanted but did not need
She will be punished for her own selfish greed

I understand
Although the pain tugs me deep
I will forgive her but I will not sleep

I PROMISE

I promise

No more licks when you sleep

but can you blame me when you taste so sweet

Trust me

I like it when I'm in too deep

I love it

When I bury my face and I can't breathe

CHAINS ON MY HEART

Chains on my wrist
Chains on my heart
Shackled to my feet
It feels like I'm locked behind bars
Physically I'm yours
Mentally I'm gone
Sexually I'm tired
of hearing your same damn moans
Some nights
I don't even want to come home
Cause' the sound of your voice
Is starting to get old
The way you lie irks my nerves
I'm dead inside
My tears are dry
I stay because I want you to change
When you don't I'm back living in the flames
and cursing your name under my breath
Why don't I leave and put us to rest

ANGELS AND DEMONS

Demon
What is he waiting for
She already played him once before
Show her you are a man
Smack her to the floor

Angel
He should not raise his hand
There is no proof of her being with another man
So there's no reason to put her on the stand

Demon
Look at him
He looks so pathetic
Thinking this woman really loves him
His faith in her is starting to give me a headache
Where does he think she's been
When she's out with her friends
Doesn't answer her phone
and when she finally comes home
She's so drunk
She pretends to have done nothing wrong
He is worthless

He let her run all over him
His stupidity makes him deserve this

Angel
Stop talking
You will not push him away
This woman has his heart and she is here to stay
He has trust and I will not let that fade
If you don't respect his judgment
Then there is nothing else to say

Demon
But listen

Angel
Enough
Do you understand
This woman made him into a man
She pulled his heart out of the dark
She took his pain and erased his scars

Demon
Listen my love
I can hear her soul

When she sleeps
She's not the same woman he wants her to be

Angel
Well, I guess we will have to wait and see
but for now stop this nonsense
Let's leave them in peace

SOMEONE TOLD ME

Someone told me
That your love wasn't worthy
That every day and night you're out doing me dirty

Someone told me
That I was a blessing
and if I am with you I will keep on stressing

Someone told me
That I was invisible
because they don't see me anymore
They think that you keep me locked indoors

Someone told me
Someone told me
Someone told me
and the list goes on
Please tell me you're not doing me wrong
and that everything they say is built around hate

SIREN

Do not look into her eyes
She will have you hypnotized
Once she makes you hers
You will fall in line
No matter how much you show her love
She will never be satisfied
When she walks her hips speak to your mind
You will kill anyone
Who tries to be deep inside
She uses your imagination
and makes all your fantasies come alive
So she can take advantage of you
and watch you slowly die
No matter how mad you get
Her voice
Will bring your heart back between her lips
and she will eat away all your pain
and suck all the blood right out of your veins
You will be too weak
To remember your own name
She uses disguises like makeup
To hide the coldness in her cheeks
She will seduce you

With sexy dresses and lingerie
To lure you into her sheets
There is no level to her madness
She will cut you deep
Have you crawling on all fours
Just to get a peek
Then put her sweetness on your tongue
and make you beg for more
She will look for attention from others
Just to piss you off
She plays with your emotions
Like a puppet on her strings
She will watch you sleep
So she can claw into your dreams
She will take all your ambitions
and make you her fiend
Love from her has never been seen
Her touch warms you up and when she goes down low
You rush to make her your Queen
but she's dangerous
A woman like her is called Siren
Take it from me
My soul's been gone
and I'm still engulfed in her sexual charms

REMEMBER ME

When I die I will not wake

My heart will stop

but my memories will never fade

My soul will live on inside heaven's gate

So please stay strong and remember my name

YOU GOT IT

You got it

I'll stay

I promise my love I will never run away

My heart is in your hands

I'll do whatever it takes to fix every part that aches

but it doesn't have to end this way

I want to live and touch you every day

I want to be with you forever

Until our bodies wither away

Just put the knife down

and I'll suffer for your mistakes

OUT OF REACH

She deserves better but you mistreat her
All she wants is love
yet you continue to deceive her
Let me ask you a question
What happens if she meets someone like me
becomes far out of your reach
and I show her love without ever dragging my feet

EMOTIONAL SCARS

There's nothing special about me
Except
I suffer from three different personalities
They all are the same
Lonely, Hurt and Drained
There's no end to this journey of pain
I'm forced to live in his madness
because I can't step out of the flames
My heart endured real emotional scars
It's hard to face my fears
When she is living right here
and I feel helpless
Trapped behind heart shaped bars
My tears rain relentlessly
Slowly making holes in my soul
That make it hard to think on my own
Sometimes I wake in the middle of the night
Eyes sore
Red from crying that afternoon at breakfast, lunch,
dinner and right before bed

FATHER

Stories have been told of my father using drugs and
them taking his soul
They said there was no stopping him
He was out of control
There was death in his eyes
and he chose to ignore the signs
From what my family told me at the age of two
He was so high he forgot I was there
I crawled to the window
Fell three stories and hit the ground
With no tears and no sound
Just blood and slow beats to my heart
I would have died
If someone did not see me
Rush to my side
and take me to the hospital
With a bit of a chance to survive
The past is the past and my pops is my pops
I do not blame him for anything
and I do not care who likes it or not
Thirty-five years went by since the fateful day
That mom took me away
By the time I saw my dad

Somehow, I recognized his face
I look just like him
There's no mistake
He told me the truth with too many graphics
It split my head in two
So I was done with asking
Half the stuff my family told me wasn't true
I know I suffer from seizures
because of that day but I love my dad
We are the perfect match

ABOUT THE AUTHOR

I was born April 29, 1983 in South Jamaica Queens, and I was raised in Staten Island. I just want my book to reach all those that have been touched by pain. Take it from me, dreams can become reality. So, no matter where you're from, never give up.

This book will show you the hard times I went through that kept me grounded. It took me this long to Publish my book, because I didn't want to be judged. Then I realized, if I ever want to make it to the top, I must come from underneath my rock, push my mind out of the box and show the world poetry is not dead.

SPECIAL THANKS

First and foremost, I would like to thank my mother and father Cookie long and Michael Johnson Sr., for making My heart what it is today.

To my brothers Keyshawn, Shaquell, Tiquan and Troy I love you even if I'm not around 24/7. I'm still here watching you all grow into men. To my sister's Priscilla, Erica, Sharon and Starr, you've all grown up to become beautiful, amazing women. Thank you all for being there every time I call. To all my nieces and nephews, too many to name, lol, I thank you for your support.

To my beautiful Fiancé Minisa Stephens, soon to be Mrs. Johnson, thank you for putting up with my madness, and for being there when I needed you the most. I love you and thank you for writing a poem in my book entitled 'Being a Woman'.

To all my uncles Keith, Stevie, Rodney and Howard I love you all. To all my aunties, Michelle, Niecey, Sharon, Finney, Deborah (RIP), Brownie, Toni Johnson and Jibber I love you all, and I thank you for keeping me in check.

Howard Long, may you rest in peace.

To the rest of my family - Johnson family, Long family and Nelsons family, Frankie, I love you. To the Finney's, Taylor, Dale, Smith, Grayson and Scott family, I love you. To the Rangers family, RIP to your mother and father, I love you. To the Booker, Coat, Walton, Briggs, and entire Baez family I love you. Tyrone, I love you bro and I'm proud of you. Rest in peace mousey. To the Browning family and to my aunt Niecey and family, may Preston find his way home soon. I miss him and the Heath family.
To the perry family, I love you all so much.

To everyone else that opened their door for me, and helped me through the struggles that I faced during my travels on this earth, I appreciate you all from every part of my soul.

RIP Storm, Cody, Michael H., and Fuquan Tilghman, I love you.

Michael Johnson, Jr.

Connect with the Author:

Tik Tok: mylifethroughpoetryeyes

Facebook: Michael Johnson (blazethepoet)

Instagram: @blazethepoet
@mylifethroughpoetryeyes

YouTube: mylifethroughpoetryeyes

Word Press: mylifethroughpoetryeyes

Email: mylifethroughpoetryeyes@gmail.com

www.ingramcontent.com/pod-product-compliance
Lightning Source LLC
Chambersburg PA
CBHW050838160426
43192CB00011B/2079